Ben of the Island

Storms and Trains

Written By: Terrilyn Kerr
Illustrated by: Nancy Perkins

ISBN: 978-1-987852-32-5

First printing June 2021

Author: Terrilyn Kerr; terrilynkerr@gmail.com; www.terrilynkerr.ca

Illustrator: Nancy Perkins; nancyperkinspainter@hotmail.com

Publisher: Wood Island Prints; 670 Trans-Canada Highway, Route 1; Wood Islands, PE C0A 1R0; (902) 962-3335; schultz@pei.sympatico.ca; www.woodislandsprints.com

This is Terrilyn Kerr`s fifth published children`s book. She lives on Prince Edward Island and writes short stories and poetry besides teaching traditional rug braiding. Terrilyn is inspired daily by the wildlife and sounds of the ocean as she walks the beaches of her beautiful Island home.

Nancy Perkins for many decades has been a painter of mainly nautical themes, working in oils and acrylics. Her work is in Island galleries, private collections and is included in the PEI Provincial Art Bank. She too lives on Prince Edward Island and has collaborated with Terrilyn on three other books.

Dedication

This book is dedicated to lighthouses everywhere and the men and women who work in them. They keep the lights burning brightly as a safeguard to all passing ships which may otherwise be dashed upon the rocks.

Once again, this book takes historical facts and blends them with fictional characters. The early schools, the storms and the coming of the trains to Prince Edward Island are all part of the history of this beautiful Island.

Nancy Perkins has been instrumental in the success of these books and I couldn`t have succeeded without her. Thank you.

Thank you to my family for their support and to my husband, Sandy for his editorial skills, encouragement and love.

Last but not least, a warm thank you to J. D. Kerr who read and edited the final copy of this book. I am blessed with friends and family.

Terrilyn Kerr

After the adventures of the Ice Boats and the Phantom Ship, Ben was still happily living at the Wood Islands Lighthouse. The community was growing, with more people moving to the area and small farms popping up all around.

The arrival of people meant more children, which in turn meant that a school was required. Soon a one room school was built for children of all ages. A teacher was hired and she taught every grade. In the winter the schoolhouse was heated by a wood stove, with the parents contributing to the wood pile and the children helping to carry in the wood. One older student was designated to come in early each morning and light the stove to get the schoolhouse warmed up for the rest of the students. Some students only attended the school until they could read and write. They then had to leave to help their families with farming or fishing. Others, more fortunate, were able to continue until they graduated.

Ben loved visiting the school to see the children. Sometimes they would give him part of their lunch. One day while wandering up the road to the school, Ben met what he thought was a bear! He immediately went into a fighting position as he faced the huge creature. Just as he was going to attack, Ben realized that the creature was actually a large, black, furry dog! His name was Hugo and he lived on one of the new farms. Hugo told Ben that he came from a place called Newfoundland and his breed was famous for their swimming strength. Over time they became best friends. Although Ben was smaller than Hugo, he was a strong swimmer himself and the two dogs had wonderful times, swimming with the seals and porpoises.

Hugo liked Ben`s lighthouse friends and joined in the games that Ben played with the donkey. He wasn`t as fast as Ben and had to run hard to avoid being knocked over by the donkey! The goats and chicken roared with laughter as they watched the donkey gaining on Hugo!

One day as the two friends were playing on the shore close to the lighthouse, the weather began to change. The sky became dark and the wind began to freshen. Soon the waves were churning into white caps and the dogs knew they should head for home. There was a storm coming, and both Ben and Hugo were needed at their homes to help gather the other animals into the barn. Hugo said goodbye to Ben and raced up the road towards his farm. Ben rounded up the chickens, horses, cow, goats and donkey, and herded them into the barn where they would be safe.

The lighthouse keeper fastened down everything that could move. He looked out to sea where he knew there would be ships in peril as they ran before the gale, trying to reach a sheltered harbour. As the wind howled and the waves pounded the shore, the sky became black and there was nothing anyone could do until the storm had run its course. Even Ben had difficulty making his way from the barn to the lighthouse, and he hoped his friend Hugo had made it safely home to the farm.

At the height of the storm a ship foundered on the rocks, but luckily several of the crew had made it safely to shore. Before they turned towards the warmth of the lighthouse however, they saw another ship in distress. Looking closely they could see the men on board desperately looking for a way to get to shore before their ship was wrecked on the rocks. Then one of the crew on board had an idea. He tied a long rope to a barrel and tied the other end of the rope to the mast. He and another man threw the barrel overboard and watched as the wind and waves carried the barrel to the shore. The waiting men were able to grab the barrel and hold on tightly. The crew from the ship then grabbed the rope and, hand over hand, pulled themselves to safety. When all were safely ashore, they made their way to the lighthouse where they dried their clothes and were fed.

When the storm was over, the men all cautiously ventured outside. They were astonished at the devastation. Half the barn`s roof was gone and there was debris on the Wood Islands` shore from several ships that had foundered in the Northumberland Strait. The farmer up the road came to the lighthouse with Hugo and joined the lighthouse keeper, Ben and other neighbourhood men. They ran to the shore, hoping to find more survivors from the wrecked ships. They looked both ways along the shore and Ben suddenly noticed something moving on the beach. He barked and ran to where a man was lying on the rocks, moaning in pain.The men carried him to the lighthouse where the lighthouse keeper`s wife cleaned his wounds and bandaged his broken leg.

Meanwhile Ben and Hugo saw movement far out in the Strait. Even though the storm had run its course, the waves were still huge. They crashed on the shore with a violent ferocity. Both dogs didn`t hesitate as they launched into the sea, fighting the enormous waves. They swam towards the movement and found a man hanging onto a large piece of wreckage, barely alive . Both dogs swam close and the man was able to hang on to Hugo`s fur and Ben`s neck as they pulled him close to shore. The rescuers were finally able to pull him onto the sand and carry him towards the lighthouse.

As the men departed, Ben was overcome with exhaustion and he staggered towards the beach. Suddenly, a huge wave crashed over him. He was thrown onto the rocks and knocked unconscious. No one saw him go down, nor did they notice as the next wave carried him further out into the Strait. Everyone was instead focused on getting the rescued man to the lighthouse.

Hugo was shaking himself on the shore when he noticed Ben wasn`t beside him. He looked around and spotted a brown form floating in the sea. Without hesitation, Hugo launched himself back into the strait and swam as hard as he could towards that form. It was Ben! Hugo grabbed onto his exposed neck and, using the last of his strength, pulled Ben back to shore. Hugo barked and barked until the lighthouse keeper looked back and saw Ben lying on the sand. He ran back to Ben and pumped his chest several times until, finally, Ben coughed up some seawater and began breathing again. Hugo was elated and danced around on the sand. They carried Ben to the lighthouse where he quickly recovered. Both dogs were celebrated as heroes that day!

The next day Ben and Hugo were walking along the beach when they heard a small whimpering noise. They searched in the crevasses of the rocks and soon came across a small, black puppy wedged in between two large rocks and covered with seaweed. They gently pried the puppy out of the rocks and carried it home to the lighthouse. The lighthouse keeper`s wife wrapped the female puppy in a soft blanket, gave her some warm milk and she fell asleep. The keeper`s wife decided to keep the pup and call her Mathilda or Matty. Both Ben and Hugo were surprised to see a girl dog in their midst. Except for their sisters as puppies, they hadn`t seen a girl dog in their neighbourhood before.

Over the next few weeks as Matty became stronger, Ben was allowed to take her outside with him. At first Hugo didn`t like her much because she had needle-like puppy teeth that she sank into his haunch, which made him yelp with pain. Then one day when Ben was dozing in the sun, she ran over and bit Ben`s ear. He let out a great howl and she fled to the barn and hid. Hugo laughed at the sight of the pup peeking out from behind the barn door, glad she`d sunk her teeth into Ben and not into him!

The months passed and the puppy grew into a gentle, intelligent dog and became good friends with both Ben and Hugo. They conveniently forgot all about her puppy teeth and enjoyed many adventures together.

Autumn came and went and soon winter was upon them. One cold winter`s night as Ben and Matty lay in front of the wood stove, Ben heard the lighthouse keeper and his wife talking about something called a train. Apparently the construction crews had completed the train tracks eastward to Murray River and Murray Harbour, and tomorrow the train would be able to stop in those villages. Ben had no idea what a train was and he was puzzled to learn that the keeper`s mother was coming for Christmas on the train. What was a train? Was it several horses pulling a wagon? Was it a type of ship? Ben had no idea so he was excited to hear that he was going to be allowed to go with the lighthouse keeper when he picked up his mother. Early the next morning the lighthouse keeper hitched up the horses, loaded extra blankets into the wagon, and called for Ben to jump in.

They set off towards the train station in Murray River, and Ben snuggled into the blankets. As they neared the railway station, Ben saw the station building and a set of iron tracks that went off into the distance. He couldn`t see anything that might be a "train" though, and wondered where it was.

Then from far away, he heard a noise like a huge whistle. It got louder and louder and soon the air was filled with a sound that was more deafening than anything Ben had ever heard. He was terrified! Soon he saw what looked like a huge apparition coming towards them at great speed, with smoke and sparks shooting out of it. Ben didn`t know where to hide! He expected the lighthouse keeper to run away, but he was just standing there with a smile on his face.

Ben cowered behind him and was surprised when a huge metal machine began to slow down and then stop in front of the station. Of course it was the train, a coal burning steam engine pulling several passenger cars and freight cars full of supplies for the towns along its route.

Out of one of the passenger cars stepped the lighthouse keeper's mother.

Ben liked her immediately because she made such a fuss over him, and insisted that he ride up on the bench with her back to the lighthouse. She wrapped him a blanket and he was toasty warm all the way home. He thought about the train and could hardly wait to tell Matty and Hugo all about it. They wouldn`t believe his description of the noise, smoke and sparks coming from the train engine.

Well, time passed and the three dogs would often be seen playing in the fields and on the beach. Matty was soon all grown up and able to help Ben shepherd the lighthouse animals, and guard them from the black bear and the lynx in the area. Hugo would still come down from his farm when he had free time from his chores.

Sometime later in the spring, Ben and Hugo started to notice that Matty had begun to change. She no longer wanted to go very far from the lighthouse or play in the fields with them. If they teased her she would snap at them and want to be left alone. After several weeks of weird behaviour, she suddenly disappeared and they couldn`t find her anywhere. Now they were worried and they spent the day frantically searching the barn, the fields, under bushes, and the beach.

When evening came and Hugo went home, Ben went to find the lighthouse keeper's wife. He wanted somehow to tell her that Matty had disappeared. The keeper`s wife was in the kitchen making dinner, and as he whined and paced, she understood what was bothering him. She smiled and took him to the space under the stairs and there was Matty lying on a pile of blankets. Ben was so very glad to see her but soon discovered that she wasn`t alone! There, nestled beside her, were four black puppies and, almost hidden, a little brown one. The brown one was so small and Ben heard the keeper`s wife call him a "runt". As Ben stood there in amazement, the keeper`s wife lifted the brown one up, wrapped him in a towel and fed him from a bottle. He heard her say that this little pup reminded her of another brown "runt" that had been born many years ago. She said that this little puppy was the spitting image of that other "runt". Of course she was speaking of Ben`s birth. She was confident that this pup would grow up to be a strong, intelligent Chesapeake Bay Retriever just like his father Ben, who was now sitting proudly beside his family.

Chesapeake Bay Retrievers *(Encyclopedia Britannica)* trace their history to two pups who were rescued from a foundering ship in Maryland in 1807. The male "Sailor" and female "Canton" were described as Newfoundland dogs, but were more accurately Lesser Newfoundland or St. John's water dogs.

The Chesapeake Bay Retriever is a large-sized breed of dog belonging to the Retriever, Gundog, and Sporting breed groups. The breed was developed in the United States Chesapeake Bay area during the 19th century. Historically used by area market hunters to retrieve waterfowl, pull fishing nets, and rescue fishermen, it is today primarily a family pet and hunting companion. They are often known for their love of water and their ability to hunt. It is a medium to large sized dog similar in appearance to the Labrador Retriever. The Chesapeake has a wavy coat, rather than the Labrador's smooth coat. They are described as having a bright and happy disposition, courage, willingness to work, alertness, intelligence, and love of water as some of their characteristics.

Newfoundland Dog *(Wikipedia)* originated in Newfoundland, and is descended from a dog landrace indigenous to the island known as the lesser Newfoundland, or St. John's water dog. Genome analysis indicates that Newfoundlands are related to the Irish water spaniel, Labrador Retriever, and Curly-Coated Retriever. The Newfoundland is a large working dog. They can be black, brown, grey, or white-and-black. However, in the Dominion of Newfoundland, before it became part of the confederation of Canada, only black and Landseer coloured dogs were considered to be proper members of the breed. They were originally bred and used as working dogs for fishermen in Newfoundland. Newfoundlands are known for their giant size, intelligence, tremendous strength, calm dispositions, and loyalty. They excel at water rescue/life saving because of their muscular build, thick double coat, webbed paws, and swimming abilities.

Labrador Retriever, a breed of sporting dog that originated in Newfoundland and was brought to England by fishermen about 1800. It is an outstanding gun dog, consistently dominating field trials. Standing 21.5 to 24.5 inches (55 to 62 cm) and weighing 55 to 80 pounds (25 to 36 kg), it is more solidly built than other retrievers and has shorter legs. Distinctive features include its otter tail, thick at the base and tapered toward the end, and its short, dense coat of black, brown ("chocolate"), or yellow. The Labrador retriever is characteristically rugged, even-tempered, and gentle. In England it has been used in military and police work, as a rescue dog, and as a guide dog for the blind. An ideal family pet, the Labrador retriever became in the 1990s the most popular dog breed in the United States.

The great August Gale of 1873 *(The August gale and the arc of memory on PEI; E MacDonald - The Island Magazine, 2004 - islandscholar.ca)* On 24 August 1873, a full-fledged Atlantic hurricane crashed ashore in Maritime Canada with devastating consequences. It was known as the August Gale, and it would be the second worst natural disaster in Island history. Yet today it is virtually forgotten in this province. After the well known "Yankee Gale" of 1851, a generation later, it all happened again. On Sunday, 24 August 1873, a full-fledged Atlantic hurricane crashed ashore in Maritime Canada, wreaking havoc on land and sea. Like the Yankee Gale, the August Gale was a devastating nor`easter, although the wind was more nearly north this time. This time there was more warning for seafarers, but though far fewer ships were caught on a lee shore than in the Yankee Gale, the magnitude of the storm defeated most precautions. Many vessels were driven from supposedly safe anchorages or ran out of sea room and were wrecked on Maritime coasts. According to one report, 1,032 vessels, including 435 small fishing schooners, were "known to have been destroyed in the neighbourhood of the Transcription from diary attributed to James F. Macnutt, Malpeque, Earle Lockerby, Fredericton, to Edward MacDonald, August 14, 2001. Henry Wolsey Bayfield, The St. Lawrence Survey Journals of Captain Henry Wolsey Bayfield, 1829–1853, vol. 2 (Toronto: Champlain Society, 1984). Haszard`s Gazette (October 21, 1851) reported one wreck and damage to vessels at Richibucto, the only published record of serious damage elsewhere. Diary of Francis Bain, entry for 24–25 August 1873. Bain, a naturalist and close observer of nature living near Charlottetown, recorded the wind at the storm`s height as one degree east of north. The Dalhousie Review Gulf of St. Lawrence and the Atlantic shores of Nova Scotia, Cape Breton and Newfoundland." The reported number of deaths was 223, although the study conceded that 500 would be a more accurate figure. On Prince Edward Island, far fewer vessels were lost (25–35) than in the Yankee Gale, but the crews were proportionally larger, and the death toll, 115–150 lives, came well within echo of the earlier disaster. Reflecting both the pattern of shipping and, probably, the August Gale`s size and track, the pattern of shipwrecks was more dispersed on Prince Edward Island than in the Yankee Gale. While a number of wrecks came ashore along the waist of the Island between Alberton and Tracadie Bay, there was a cluster of wrecks at both extremities of the province, as vessels tried vainly to weather either East Point or North Cape. The losses there were mostly fishing schooners, but along the North Shore the wrecks included a number of large cargo vessels. In contrast to the Yankee

Gale, storm damage in 1873 also extended to the south side of the Island. There was local flooding in the east end of Charlottetown, where the storm surge washed away the newly constructed railway embankment, and all along the South Shore wharves were battered, and vessels driven from their moorings.

The Prince Edward Island Railway (PEIR) *(PE Archival Facts)* was an historic Canadian railway in Prince Edward Island (PEI). The railway ran tip-to-tip on the island, from Tignish in the west to Elmira in the east, with major spurs serving Borden-Carleton's train ferry dock, the capital in Charlottetown, Montague and Georgetown and the original eastern terminus at Souris. A major spur from Charlottetown served Murray River and Harbour on the south coast.

Construction began in 1871 but costs almost bankrupted the government by the next year, a problem that helped pave PEI's entrance into Confederation. The work was picked up by the Canadian Government Railways and largely completed by the mid-1880s. The PEIR saw heavy use, especially during World War II, but like many railways saw declining use through the 1970s. The line officially closed on 31 December 1989 and the rails removed between 1990 and 1992, with the provincial government receiving a one-time payment of $200 million to upgrade the road network in exchange for not opposing the closure.

The provincial government purchased the properties in 1994, and 75 percent of the route now forms the basis of the Confederation Trail rail trail system. The station in Elmira at the eastern end of the line is now used as the Elmira Railway Museum.